Lockdown Poetry

Life With Poetry

Chloe Gilholy

Published by Chloe Gilholy, 2021.

LOCKDOWN POETRY

First edition. August 1, 2021.

Written by Chloe Gilholy.

Table of Contents

Topsy-Turvy Love 1
Lettuce Think...2
Late Night Call 4
Referral 5
Depeche 6
Heroine of Our Time 7
Purple Shines Bright 9
Unexplained 10
The Feeling...12
13 Days Of Halloween 13
I Miss it 17
Ship of Fools 19
Joe & Ivy 20
25 Years 21
Mountains & Gems..23
I Want 24
Spirit in Shatters 25
Spiked Drinks...26
Ode to Summer Love..27
Summer Monster 28
Haikubes Review 29
Moscow Winter 31
Lady of Acid...32
Tale of Two Flowerpots..33
Game Rage 34
Cake..35
Here's What I Observed..36
Cake Ache 37
Strawberry..38
Fish 39
Soup...40

Apple 41

Halo-Halo 42

Pancake 43

Gold & White Beaches 44

She, Lady Vengeance 45

Hell-bent Waters 46

Gorgeous Forests 47

Mr Alphabet's Pets 48

Raven's Day Out 50

First to The Bar 51

Malibu Milk 52

Nostalgic Holidays 53

Dehumanized 55

Mini Arcade Machine 56

Cycle 57

Dolphin 58

Some Good Advice 59

This is my world now 60

No One Ever Let Me Know 61

Escape Your Fate 62

Grateful 63

Good Morning God 64

Ciao With Marrowbone 66

Peace And Goodwill In The Universe 68

The Alcoholic Alphabet 70

Vintage Swing 73

Three Things 74

Giant Leaves 75

Happy Ending 76

Pålegg 77

The Elderly Painter 78

Why it's Grey 79

We Walked 80

The Flowers of Suicide Forest 81

Diet Pills In The View Of An Atheist 83

Love is all full...84

Mother Fluff Was A Diamond..85

They Rose 86

Lush Life 87

Blue smiles..88

Back to Work..89

Pink Smiles..90

Goddamn Perverts 91

Your Game Is Lame 92

What People Think Of Writers 93

A Standoff...94

Red Bubbles 95

Long Live the Paper Queen..96

Sundays 97

Haikus..98

Heart-Shaped Glasses 99

Pets.. 100

Friday Fries 101

How I Can Be A Better Person 103

An Open Book... 104

Jungle Influencers 105

Topsy-Turvy Love

Through my tainted eyes, it's always snowy;
    Tropical skies, a true topsy-turvy.
    Is there blood on my cheeks? No need for fears,
    The mud on my face: It must be my tears.
    My self-esteem taught me I was ugly,
    On goes the face filters – now I'm pretty
    With a storm of hearts and pixie dust.
    Like one of the tarts, I'm his one true lust.
    Fire soaring, stripped beige; it's getting fruitful,
    Like we never age; I feel beautiful!
    He bathes me in his neon fantasies:
    Turns them into vibrant realities.

Lettuce Think

How can people afford fountains of booze
    But have no time for a bath or shower?
    I really wish I was on that cruise.
    The odor is horrific at any hour.
    This establishment is faulty;
    Cheap entry and counterfeit goods.
    At least there's cards against humanity
    Though we'd have have more fun in the woods.
    "The money is missing!"
    Cried one of the volunteers.
    Then I see what someone is cradling...
    Never seen anything like it in years.
    The pub quiz was interrupted
    By a free giveaway
    I see my team get frustrated
    They just want to play
    "Who wants some lettuce?"
    Crowds jumped and arms reached out!
    I heard someone say, "Get hit by a bus!"
    I don't know what that was all about.
    We won that quiz despite the issues
    We went to reception to claim our prize:
    The staff all looked like they needed tissues
    They let us have it which was a surprise.

So we know where the charity money went
Not to Oxfam, or Children in Need
Well this is well and truly bent
Well what a load of bollocks indeed.
We hopped to the bar with much less dread
The lettuce munchers made me stop to think
My friends tapped my shoulder and said;
"Come on and pick a drink!"
Everything afterwards is green and blurred
Stale salad, cold curry and tea for breakfast,
With a red rose it's all been stirred...
This will take some time to adjust.

Late Night Call

There's nothing like seducing an old friend
    at two o'clock in the morning only to find
    he had plans for me all this time, and was
    waiting for the Queen to make her move.

Referral

You've got to be told; you'll never understand!
    Don't reach out! Don't you dare touch my hand.
    I've met knights like you in white suits many times before;
    Twirling pens, polished shoes and thick notes about some whore.
    They'll infect you like they've infected me: the parasites!
    Breed hate and breathe despair on sleepless nights.
    Even in a state of coma, there is no escape.
    The master of illness smiles in his cape.
    Chronic downfalls, partially deaf, partially blind, manic depression,
    Labels slapped, tickets punched, institution after institution.
    They ask you what is wrong, and you cannot explain –
    Your only companion is the howling of the rain...
    Bad days turn to stressful weeks as the tears crust.
    Pleasant memories discarded in beds of dust.
    So, I leave a note for the fly on the wall – my little spy
    If you wish to see the world with my eyes – kiss the sun goodbye...

Depeche

Speak and spell a broken frame
    It's construction time again
    For some great reward
    It's a black celebration
    With music for the masses
    Featuring the violator with
    Songs of faith and devotion
    I am the ultra exciter
    Playing the angel with
    Sounds of the universe
    Through the delta machine's spirit

Heroine of Our Time

She smiles in the corner
    Pen behind her ear
    Book by her chin
    She'll grow up
    Cool and cunning
    Surrounded by wealth
    She's poor now
    But spiritually
    Is a millionaire
    She studies women
    History never forget
    Entrepreneurs galore
    Queens of Hollywood
    Writing sisters and
    A virgin queen
    They say it's a tragedy
    That they never had
    Stable husbands nor children
    To the first day in class
    To the final exam results
    She's learned to take her own path
    She vows to be free
    From expectations and
    Embrace life on her own terms

She's done her best
She has no regrets
The heroine of our time

Purple Shines Bright

Myself and the world wish you
the greatest birthday you ever had,
and even greater ones to come.
Thank you for the smiles, and for
giving light to the new generation
when the future seems bleak.
Thank you for your voice, the music
the kindness, and the hard work,
and all the love you give to your fans.
You've fixed black and broken hearts
We now have purple hearts in this tribe
And purple shines bright.
This tribe that we call a fandom, we may be
divided by oceans and languages, but we united
by a passion for music that you bring to life.
May you shine brightly in this life,
and the next one, wherever it may
take you... it's bound to be great.

Unexplained

An overload of information, in one ear and out the other
     scattered all over the place like flakes of dust.
     The dead flies decaying on the ground...
     are the happy thoughts forgotten.
     Anxious to ask the questions,
     I can't shake the fear of scalding,
     In case they think I'm stupid...
     I can't seem to do anything right.
     All I ever hear is moaning.
     Is it worth the risk?
     All around me are red flags,
     Constant oppression and little demons
     They call me ugly in the mirror!
     Taunt me in photographs!
     Critique everything I do!
     What is there to look forward to?
     Nobody wants to listen.
     They would never understand.
     I just feel so empty all the time.
     Though little things the emptiness is refilled,
     there's a gaping hole in my smile.
     the emptiness returns quickly all the knowledge I have is
imprisoned.
     I know it's going to get worse as the years go on

I want it all, but I can't have it all.
Scribbles upon wet pages...
Suffer to live.
I want to live, but I must die.
I want to die, but I must live.

The Feeling

Whilst we're drowned in scandals, that
    OUR neighbours succumb to darkness.
    We find ourselves in it too.
    Full of black clouds and dust,
    It's easy to think that we are alone.
    Following the rays from the other side,
    I escape one maze and fall into another.
    Roasted by the sun, melting to the floor.
    Chilled by the moon, body tangled.
    The nature that we love also kills us.
    We see our neighbours as rivals.
    We see our doorsteps as borders.
    Simple things scare me
    Despite once climbing mountains,
    Imprinting footsteps onto sands,
    Breathing in Norwegian fjords.
    I have depression.
    But people don't know it.
    They won't accept it.
    All they see is fake smiles.
    It's just another
    obstacle to overcome

13 Days Of Halloween

On the first day of Halloween
    Dracula gave to me:
    A casket in an organ!
    On the second day of Halloween
    Dracula gave to me:
    Two white dresses,
    And a casket in an organ!
    On the third day of Halloween
    Dracula gave to me:
    Three black cats;
    Two white dresses,
    And a casket in an organ!
    On the fourth day of Halloween
    Dracula gave to me:
    Four screeching bats;
    Three black cats;
    Two white dresses,
    And a casket in an organ!
    On the fifth day of Halloween
    Dracula gave to me:
    Five spell books;
    Four screeching bats;
    Three black cats;
    Two white dresses,

And a casket in an organ!
On the sixth day of Halloween
Dracula gave to me:
Six pumpkin spice lattes;
Five spell books;
Four screeching bats;
Three black cats;
Two white dresses,
And a casket in an organ!
On the seventh day of Halloween
Dracula gave to me:
Seven metal albums;
Six pumpkin spice lattes;
Five spell books;
Four screeching bats;
Three black cats;
Two white dresses,
And a casket in an organ!
On the eighth day of Halloween
Dracula gave to me:
Eight sizzling cauldrons;
Seven metal albums;
Six pumpkin spice lattes;
Five spell books;
Four screeching bats;
Three black cats;
Two white dresses,
And a casket in an organ!
On the ninth day of Halloween
Dracula gave to me:
Nine zombies swinging;
Eight sizzling cauldrons;

Seven metal albums;
Six pumpkin spice lattes;
Five spell books;
Four screeching bats;
Three black cats;
Two white dresses,
And a casket in an organ!
On the tenth day of Halloween
Dracula gave to me:
Ten goblins grooving;
Nine zombies swinging;
Eight sizzling cauldrons;
Seven metal albums;
Six pumpkin spice lattes;
Five spell books;
Four screeching bats;
Three black cats;
Two white dresses,
And a casket in an organ!
On the eleventh day of Halloween
Dracula gave to me:
Eleven dragons slaying;
Ten goblins grooving;
Nine zombies swinging;
Eight sizzling cauldrons;
Seven metal albums;
Six pumpkin spice lattes;
Five spell books;
Four screeching bats;
Three black cats;
Two white dresses,
And a casket in an organ!

On the twelfth day of Halloween
Dracula gave to me:
Twelve ghosts hosting;
Eleven dragons slaying;
Ten goblins grooving;
Nine zombies swinging;
Eight sizzling cauldrons;
Seven metal albums;
Six pumpkin spice lattes;
Five spell books;
Four screeching bats;
Three black cats;
Two white dresses,
And a casket in an organ!
On the thirteenth day of Halloween
Dracula gave to me:
Thirteen skeletons singing;
Twelve ghosts hosting;
Eleven dragons slaying;
Ten goblins grooving;
Nine zombies swinging;
Eight sizzling cauldrons;
Seven metal albums;
Six pumpkin spice lattes;
Five spell books;
Four screeching bats;
Three black cats;
Two white dresses,
And a casket in an organ!

I Miss it

I miss it - the madness!
    Who would have thought,
    That I, so desperate to escape,
    extreme hunger for sanity,
    that doesn't exist embraces
    velvet insanity
    I had goals - the boredom
    I stopped the faucet and
    and fixed the organs
    nothing else
    to moan about
    nothing worth
    fighting for
    no justice to seek
    no reason to weep
    it sleeps in a corner
    growing stronger
    it will come to a point
    where fighting
    will be
    futile
    I have no fairy tales to write
    I've never had a happily ever after
    of my own

All these words of mine
form tales of sin and treachery.
We always cause the ones we love
the most pain.
No matter how many times
I say I will be okay...
Sometimes... it's hard to believe myself
I should be happy
but I'm not!
For what am I?
A lost doll with fragile tears...

Ship of Fools

It was the businessman's second honeymoon.
    His opal suite, the grandest cabin of them all.
    Daffodils at HIS balcony – nod at the lagoon.
    His wife returns from a library brawl.
    He thought the deprived spirits were gone...
    Until the Captain was butchered up the stairs.
    Husband and wife had no God to pray on,
For the crew had deathly coloured stairs.
    A housewife poisons her only child: a son.
    Regrets it as his last words are: I'm going to be a father.
    Her lover drowns before a mermaid in the sun.
    The ghosts embrace the scarlet lather...
    The housewife surrendered as the ship of fools sunk.
    The survivors fled. Memories concealed in a trunk.

Joe & Ivy

Poor Mr Joe Davis
    No matter how hard he tries
    He can't stop sinking into the abyss
    Where nobody hears his cries
    His life slips through his fingers
    Swallowed by the devil's brands
    The monster still lingers
    On his bloody hands
    Poor Mrs Ivy Davis
    A Swedish babe barely thirty
    Oblivious to her own bliss
    Vomiting her natural beauty
    An obsession with anorexic art
    She turns to her friend Bulimia
    It drives the sweethearts apart
    But Joe always had a grotesque idea
    If the paintings could talk
    And the rotten flesh write
    All the secrets would begin to walk
    To the Queen of Maggot's delight
    Joe plans Ivy's rebirth with glee
    His quiet haven truly disturbs
    His executioner is the cat lady
    who gives him what he deserves

25 Years

25 years of marriage
    Even wearing bulky armour
    And having a dash of moonlight
    I'm always the runner-up
    Mist beneath the smoky embers
    Atomic number: 47
    Toxic heavy metal
    Sterling iron mountains
    Baby hippos above
    the pebbles handing out
    Chinese imports
    AG: French argent
    Chemical element: German Silber
    Metal: Italian argento
    Symphonic: Maltese fidda
    Period element: Portuguese prata
    Soft: Zulu esilva
    Thermal: Filipino pilak
    Reflective: Japanese gin
    Antique: Indonesian perak
    Celebrating and remembering
    The death of the king
    Childhood in 8-bit graphics
    Quarter of a century

The pile of dimes cashed in
At the lustrous bank
25 years on the throne

Mountains & Gems

I want
     mountains & gems
     with no
     strings attached.
     I'll take
     the lovers
     with
     fat pockets.
     I'm sorry
     in advance;
     your tears
     are delicious!

I Want

I want to wake
    to the smell of tulips
    lie back in jewels
    and laugh
    I want to pour out
    DANCE under flapping crows
    wind flowing over
    toes to the sky
    I drink sunshine
    in little tubs
    wobbling and reeling
    by the window
    I want to wash
    my flaws in
    narcissus waters
    green-white beryl floats
    Then lie some more
    in sunspots
    sniffing green fragrances

Spirit in Shatters

spirit in shatters
    bottles empty, drug count low
    i want some vodka
    all in my wallet
    is cannabis and crackers
    can't find my bank card
    they call me lazy
    they think i am sponger
    everyday struggles
    stop committing crime
    says the man with the blue badge
    go and get a job
    there are days when i
    scream, balance disturbed with the
    constant changes seen
    i know i am ill
    it's painfully obvious
    i dread the labels
    body in one piece
    organs and bones working fine
    i have mind cancer
    please prime minister
    please don't ban, i need these drugs
    the cancer will spread

Spiked Drinks

No ceiling near; the pure high air is fat,
 Glide silently near clouds without a sigh,
 A neon world below your weary cat,
 You cannot hope to know until you cry,
 Your life's a bore; absorb the gentle trust,
 Try your luck and chance, the rewards are nice
 Your life's a chore; believe in the black lust
 Buy a new romance and kiss them all twice
 Nobody sees the shining heart within,
 The crumbs of love locked in a fancy cage,
 Now leave behind a life that's closing in,
 Open the book of bondage; turn the page,
 Your silver locket dazzles through the night,
 Sky high, never surrender in your flight.

Ode to Summer Love

My sharp boyfriend, you inspire me to write.
    How I love the way you cuddle and drink,
    Invading my mind day and through the night,
    Always dreaming about the fun eye blink.
    Let me compare you to a shiny sky?
    You are more awesome, perfect and caring.
    Smooth drought dries the dun picnics of July,
    And summertime has the one childbearing.
    How do I love you? Let me count the ways.
    I love your darling fingers, style and smile.
    Thinking of your glaring style fills my days.
    My love for you is the staring profile.
    Now I must away with a subject heart,
    Remember my smart words whilst we're apart.

Summer Monster

My round monster, you inspire me to write.
  I hate the way you bark, wallow and sting,
  Invading my mind day and through the night,
  Always dreaming about the gruesome fling.
  Let me compare you to a bluff buffoon?
  You are more loathsome, amusing and rough.
  Buff sun heats the bruising peaches of June,
  And summertime has the musing LeBoeuf.
  How do I hate you? Let me count the ways.
  I hate your eyes, toenails and eyelashes.
  Thinking of your tough toenails haunts my days.
  My hate for you is the benign hashes.
  Now I must away with a divine heart,
  Remember my bound words whilst we're apart.

Haikubes Review

How can I review
    Haikubes without turning this
    Into some haikus?
    Dices with red words
    Generate prompts and concepts
    Black words must be used.
    Sixty-three peach cubes
    Only a matter of time
    Before clones follow
    In a half-green box:
    Social entertainment for
    Coffee table nights!
    For many years this
    Gathered dust on my bookshelves
    "What is this?" They asked?
    Haikus by Haikubes
    "Tragic effort! Craft your own!"
    A customer says.
    Haikus for Christmas
    Cubes rolled, scattered, then married
    Off as poetry.
    Leaving your fate in
    The hands of peculiar
    Dice is limiting

I do like this game.
Expensive for what it is.
haikus brings me peace.
A thumbs up from me
Good fun for thirty minutes
I crown it three stars!

Moscow Winter

It's always snowing in a Moscow winter
    That's what they always said to me
    It's something I would have like to have seen,
    But I wouldn't know as I've never been
    Past the candy temples and twirled rooftops
    It's not my Instagram that captured the moment
    Of white trees, deep footprints and marble skies.
    I've heard the tales of Russian spies and agents
    Scattered in stories old and new
    It makes me think of
    What lovely landscapes are spoilt by carbon mismanagement
    There's always somebody or something
    That spoils the wonderful works of human and Mother Nature
    We hear many things about the things in Russia
    The good and the bad
    But all countries are like that in their own way
    I still want to go and set my own mark there.

Lady of Acid

Hajimemashite!
  I'm the Lady of Acid.
  Here you go, have some Prima Donna oddity,
  Because it makes up for my lack of sanity.
  Come on in.
  Take your shoes off.
  Make yourself at home;
  You're just in time for lunch.
  Sweet leaf and goldfish:
  What an odd dish indeed.
  It's okay, cause vibrating tea
  Makes everything so yummy.
  Invaders are digging...
  Every box with a pearl.
  I promise, Mr Officer:
  I had no coke!
  Please be gentle with me,
  I have nothing to hide...
  Now don't be so alarmed.
  I have a funny feeling
  That your milk bottle's going to explode!

Tale of Two Flowerpots

There was once two little flower pots:
    The one on the right had valiant red pansies,
    The one on the left had noble purple pansies.
    Both came from a shop that I love lots and lots.
    England is known for its summer rain.
    Why is there snow wreaking havoc in April?
    Why are plants dying from frost in April?
    I hope watering them every day isn't in vain.
    There was just one red pansy standing.
    Then the next day there two, and then three pops up.
    Little by little, the flowerpot became full as more stood up.
    The red pansies are great at surviving.
    Tragedy struck for the purple pansies,
    As the petal shrivelled like the end of the ball.
    To get these crisp dead flowers to be once again tall,
    Would take a miracle in strong degrees.
    One splash could not feed all.

Game Rage

Oh my god! That is bullshit!
Where the fuck did that blue shell come from?
I am clearly the best racer of all time!
Fuck off Caterpie: nobody likes you.
Come back when you're all grown up.
Tell your shiny friends to jump out the grass.
What? My turnips are only worth 20 bells?
You made my Facebook friend a millionaire.
Now I've got to change the time again.
Did you just use Kirbycide on me again?
My fighter has boobs, I should win by default!
I am not losing to these cheap bastards.
Error connection? Fuck off! My internet is perfect.
I did not buy a catalogue of error code messages.
SORT YOUR SERVERS OUT!
What? Battery low? No it isn't!
I just charged my console five minutes ago.
Stupid game! JUST LET ME WIN!

Cake

I can't bake cakes worthy of a celebration.
    Where are all the rainbows Instgram promised me?
    The hues are duller than the advertised poster.
    These baking artists have absolute devotion.
    We are told that cake is full of fat and sugar,
    Some have creamy layers, fruits engraved with chocolate,
    Some are simple, bread-based, or had crumbly layers.
    Some sophisticated cakes even have liquor.
    Supermarkets hosted caterpillar bake offs.
    This is a passage of rite for the young children.
    Cuthbert had worn the crown in pride for thirty years.
    Colin, Clyde, Wiggles and Morris were quite well-scoffed.
    And as they always say at the end of the day,
    It does not matter that the cake is not gourmet.

Here's What I Observed

Here's what I've observed...
    Geeks in green glasses working as slaves
    are beautiful Greeks eating like kings.
    Magnolia garments disposed in fire,
    replaced by flawless frocks stitched by the empire.
    I have a diploma in being a fly on the wall,
    and a master's degree as a professional spy.
    If only they've embraced
    the beautiful quirks, and see
    What would have been
    had there have been courage.
    Some correlations are destined to work:
    Bread and butter.
    Many should never be mixed:
    Booze and politics.
    Loyalty is the secret to immortality.
    Disloyalty always paves a tragic path.
    Those dying snakes in front of us were once human.

Cake Ache

I had two birthday cakes:
    One nut free from Tesco, yellow and sugary
    One baked by a friend with
    purple swirls and strawberry halves
    After one week living off cake and tea
    I returned to work and there
    cake galore from all over the world
    Cinnamon swirls, rice puddings,
    slices with so much rum you could get drunk
    When I got back I had
    a cheesecake to take home.
    The evidence had long since gone
    My tummy ached for days but
    My waistline was saved
    by vigorous swimming and gym sessions.

Strawberry

A fresh strawberry from the summer trees
    Are red, ripe and no longer green.
    This one was handpicked to be
    Washed, sliced, diced and blended
    With whole milk, whipped cream and
    bananas for a beautiful milkshake!
    Another strawberry freshly sprout
    Is another that's about to come out.
    It dosen't really give a damn
    That it's going to be damson jam.
    The old strawberries, withered and dry
    Is not destined to become compost just yet
    It's figure is preserved as it forms an orchestra
    With raisins, apricots, and oat clusters.
    They call their band, granola.

Fish

The catch of the day is the feast of tomorrow
    The wet smell from the market lingers
    In fish pies, sushi bars and chip shops
    The catch of the day is the banquet of tomorrow.
    Hanging by their fins inhaling smoke
    They don't look appetizing when raw
    I never thought I would like eating fish
    Hanging by their fins inhaling smoke
    Their home was a large ocean
    linked by streaming rivers and crashing waterfalls
    Now they're dead, they've travelled
    Further then they ever did at sea where
    Their home was a large ocean

Soup

Starting off with winter fuel
    On a granite table nestled with
    Universal cutlery and
    Polite attire in a dining room
    Steam pours from the
    Orange liquid as the round
    Utensil dives into a vegetable
    Pool
    Spices from botanic gardens start their
    Obbligato with great maestro and even
    Unused notes and flavours are destined to
    Prosper on the tongue
    Salvation and sincerity
    Onboard a cruise ship's dining room
    Umbrella of earthy foods like
    Potato and leek
    Sharing bread rolls and butter sticks
    Ogling stacks of wine
    Under large crystal chandeliers
    Playing classical music as the boat sways
    Spending our small wages on a night of leisure
    Oxygen is being put to good use
    Unmatched by anything else
    Perfection is something rarely seen

Apple

Everybody knows the old wife's tale
 That biting into a tender apple a day
 Keeps the angelic doctor away
 It indeed counts towards the 5-a-day
 With so many apples in the world
 There's enough apples to keep me
 Counting till my dying day
 Just as many apples as there are stars
 More stars in the sky than words can say
 So much to do with all these apples
 I can craft sweet cider comforts
 Feed a house with homemade pies
 and quench thirst with fresh juice
 Apple takes many forms
 But how does an apple a day
 Keep the doctor away
 When there aren't enough of them?

Halo-Halo

This is an Asian summertime treat
    That makes you sit down and eat.
    Makes you feel good from your hair to your feet,
    It's okay to accept your dietary defeat.
    Lots of sweets, fruit and shaved ice,
    Mixed with milk and ice cream is nice.
    If there is more, you can have it twice.
    If you're hungry: have it thrice!
    If you want to feel the Filipino mood,
    It is best to know it through our food.
    With all the ingredients you must include,
    Halo-Halo is delicious I must conclude.
    And alas the pleasant taste and sweet fume,
    Makes us forget the withering gloom.
    And in a tragic world filled with doom,
    We need something to make us bloom.

Pancake

Fluffy pancakes are the best: Love the texture
    Unsung heroes of the morning in France
    For if you prefer savoury or sweet
    You can always find a pancake for you
    Paying for precious starts of the day
    at a hipster restaurant in local bistros.
    All stacked up with banana slices,
    summer fruit sauce, and lemon muster.
    No, I must never underestimate
    the diversity of pancakes.
    Calling one of the many times
    I flew to another continent:
    A neon diner in New York serves
    pancakes with bacon and thick syrup
    Kleve also has lovely spots for brunch,
    among other things,
    Even for the baby Dutch pancakes,
    although it's a city in Germany.

Gold & White Beaches

Gold and white beaches is where she will twirl
    For her audience: a lonesome cocoon.
    He wants to play with his favourite pearl,
    Beneath the surface of a mauve lagoon.
    The oyster is free with three fingers in.
    At last! The bedtime story shall begin.
    He kissed her two pretty little seashells.
    She surfed in, dropping her fragile defence,
    Massaged his palms against the wedding bells.
    Souls connected; she devours his essence.
    Cruel Destiny did not make her aware
    That a cancer will cut short her affair.
    All the evidence she has, washed away...
    To memories of a hot summer's day...

She, Lady Vengeance

It was the march of the black queen!
　　She knew only to kill or be killed.
　　She was once betrothed to a wealthy lord.
　　He promised her the eternal happiness.
　　He married his mistress, took her land
　　And left her in a ditch to die.
　　On the full moon, she rose
　　Nursed by the commoners who worshipped her.
　　She borrowed a horse and spear, returned to her home
　　And slashed her traitor in his sleep.
　　Tears of rage erupted, then was deafened
　　My a mellow meows in the corner of the room.
　　Here comes the Lady Vengeance
　　Her heart thawed by four-legged beauties.

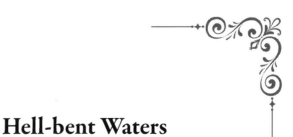

Hell-bent Waters

She's a goddess with a vision.
    He's a prince with a platinum future
    Both lather in secret dynamics
    The press adore them:
    Epitome of young love,
    Fame and success.
    But even when the cameras leave
    And the vanity is washed away
    By hell-bent waters...
    It's their affection that keeps them afloat
    A lifeguard that can't be seen.

Gorgeous Forests

These gorgeous forests scream tranquillity
    The scent of roasted marshmallows and toast,
    With guitar serenades luring singers and dancers
    Of various skills
    These peaches in look sweet and juicy
    Piled high in bowls followed by bananas,
    Strawberries, apples, raspberries and cream
    I don't know what's in the pot
    But it makes me think of India
    They welcome me in the circle
    Help yourself to some food and drink
    As the sun went down
    The blankets came out
    I went in alone
    And left with love.

Mr Alphabet's Pets

Alligators munch on
    broccoli behind the
    cabbage pack.
    Dark poisons in disguise;
    envy in their eyes.
    Frogs escape the fungus,
    greets the grapes,
    hops on herbs and
    ivy vines –
    jungle days are over!
    kiwi and kale for
    lizards sleeping on
    moss moulds
    nocturnal beings
    oozing with style
    Pepper the parrot's
    quiff sways with grace.
    She rocks her feet and
    shakes as if there's a
    tango in the cage.
    Unripe bananas and
    viridian vegetables
    wolfed down by
    Xander the monkey.

You can't miss his face!
Zachery Alphabet loves them all!

Raven's Day Out

One tired mind: aching feet, banging headache.
    Just half a head dreaming about a steak,
    The other resting on the restaurant's brink.
    Little fingers curled around the red drink.
    One gulp: one glass down. I feel all awake
    Snap of the camera turned my wine pink
    The meat feast polished. The waiter brings cake
    Sprinkled with ice creams begins to sink.
    In this crazy tour I chose to partake...
    There was no such sweet time to even blink .
    Things could be missed with just a little wink,
    Imagery that we can never remake.
    The burlesque entertainment is opaque.
    The good and the bad start to interlink.
    No clue what just happened, in any case,
    Memories will be preserved in pen's ink!

First to The Bar

I'm the first to the bar
and the last to go to bed.
The pints unleash the devil in me
and the angel within.
After ordering a fried Mars bar
and festive kebab
I'm downing crates at home
crying, "Kiss me! Kiss me!"
In morning crawls
my Celtic soul is back
I won't be possessed again – I lied!

Malibu Milk

Shots of Malibu with milk
    are simply marvellous
     It's got to be coconut milk
     It's pretty fun to make
     You can also use whole milk
     I got drunk on it in Morocco
     I love that ice fresh milk

Nostalgic Holidays

I don't want to go
    I thought we were going
    Into a pool of darkness
    I couldn't swim back then
    My first day there
    I befriended a lion
    Wearing a football shirt
    And a clown in the tower
    I didn't want to leave Blackpool
    I didn't want to go
    I thought we were going
    Into a big bath together
    I had one last night
    My first day there
    I befriended swimmers
    In a Roman bath
    I didn't want to leave Bath
    I don't want to go
    I thought we were going
    Into the mouth of a bear
    Everything scared me back then
    My first day there
    I befriended all the
    Residents in the aquarium

And a couple of shells
I didn't want to leave Bournemouth.

Dehumanized

Swinging zombies with drowned livers.
    Burning heals and tired bladders.
    Pinching Bloody Mary, slurping spirits.
    Licking mouldy kebabs
    and frozen dusk flakes with
    hanging jaws and swirling tongues.
    Flesh eating flesh: even vegans are guilty.
    Gangs crawling around a dried out crate,
    Sucking whatever they can find
    Exchanging organs and emotions
    Brawls so bad, the monkeys next door looked posh.
    Not to worry no one was harmed
    they'll be back in class tomorrow
    Just be extremely numb
    "Bunch of twats," thought the cat
    that clawed their backs.
    "How dare they eat my goods.
    I'm calling the police!"

Mini Arcade Machine

The mini arcade machine fits nicely in my hands
    I should ask the doctor if I can borrow his screwdriver
    So I can enjoy retro gaming across the lands
    I want to be the ultimate Pacman reviver
    It's small enough even for my cats
    to play with their furry paws
    If they could see maybe even bats
    They'll think I'm Santa Claus
    It's not everyday that the pint is bigger
    than the disco arcade machine
    And I'm not a fibber
    When I say I'm mean
    A mini arcade machine
    A big retro gamers dream

Cycle

The cycle will start again
    Just how it always does
    Shattered in seconds
    Fixed up again
    Following dreams
    Fixed up again
    Shattered in seconds
    Just how it always does
    The cycle will start again

Dolphin

It rose under sea
    Listen to its call
    Its like a flower
    Watch and be amazed

Some Good Advice

If it makes you sick throw it out!
    No good leaving it to mould
    If it makes you sad throw it out!
    Your heart should not be cold.
    If it makes you tired throw it out!
    You're too young to feel old.
    If it makes you feel heavy throw it out!
    Let the magic unfold.
    If it makes you angry throw it out!
    Do as you're told.

This is my world now

filled with exotic tranquillity
the path of winter's revenge
brought me no summer fruits
or the touch of autumn's peace
or the kiss of spring
i have abandoned
my hatred
my troubles
i am not your servant
my life is not your life
i live for myself
i will do what i want
when i want and how i want
this is my world now

No One Ever Let Me Know

No one ever let me know
　　About the silver snow
　　Or the winter's glow
　　It's magic that I'll never let go
　　Of in village of bow

Escape Your Fate

The only way to escape your fate is
   to triumph over sun, wind, rain and snow.
   One path to pure and everlasting bliss.
   Who knows which path is the right way to go?
   It's different for me.
   It's different for you.
   Our paths are not the same.
   Still, I am grateful that our paths have crossed.
   So make your choice.
   Which door will you open?
   One is the staircase to Heaven.
   The other is the pitfall to Hell.
   Solve the riddle
   And you will live.

Grateful

Think of a fruit when I'm away
    And keep the sweet taste in mind
    The caffeine kicks in the morning
    The chamomile wind at night
    I won't blow out the candles
    The flame represents life
    For that I am grateful

Good Morning God

Good morning, God
    Whether you're real, fake
    Or just a figure of my imagination
    is it okay to talk to you?
    Christmas is coming
    Winter's stamped her feet
    I just want to get through the day
    with fun and laughter.
    Good afternoon, God
    It's me again
    They all think I'm strange:
    I don't want the new iPhone
    or a sparkly gadget
    I don't want what's expected of me
    I just want everlasting friendship
    and quirky adventures
    Good evening, God
    I bet you're fed up with me
    I know you're busy – I am too
    I hope I'm a good Christian
    Although my friends aren't
    God speaks back
    Be patient!
    Be sweet!

Stay strong!
You're on the right path
You never annoy me
You can call back anytime

Ciao With Marrowbone

Ciao with a marrowbone,
    Tapping with my red heels.
    Hey, Billy!
    Get the oven on:
    I'm cooking sirloin steak!
    Buenos Dias with paella,
    Sneaking with my bare feet.
    Hey, Billy!
    It's time to get up:
    You're half a teacake.
    Bonjour with Cuisse de Grenouille,
    Strolling in my leather boots.
    Hey, Billy!
    Pick up your wallet:
    We're going out tonight!
    Konnichiwa with yakitori,
    Dancing in my feline slippers.
    Hey, Billy!
    Get your rod out:
    We're going fishing!
    Ni Hao with gelatine,
    Sprinting in my yellow trainers.
    Hey, Billy!
    Find the meat with the bones:

I'm going to give it a good old rub!

Peace And Goodwill In The Universe

I couldn't stop thinking about
    The ignored sign in the town.
    It Reminds me of something that
    My old man once said to me.
    He was the first and only man,
    That I ever fell in love with.
    His bedtime stories brought spice
    In my black and white world.
    Before we say our goodnights,
    He would raise his left thumb,
    And make me repeat
    The same phrase every night.
    THE UNIVERSE IS MADE OF...
    The universe is made of...
    PEACE AND GOODWILL!
    Peace and goodwill!
    Peace And Goodwill In The Universe.
    The words have been washed away:
    Replaced by celebrity hearsay
    The message has stayed in my heart.
    I've made his wisdom travel
    To my wife and kids
    The perfect message

Still falls on deaf ears

The Alcoholic Alphabet

A is for ale.
    Very light and pale.
    It's an old man's tale.
    B is for beer.
    Of course, it's got to be here.
    Always good to have one near.
    C is for cider.
    The tongue becomes a rider.
    Makes the brain go wilder.
    D is for Damascan Punch.
    Goes well with your lunch.
    The ice cubes pack a crunch.
    E is for Egg nog.
    A favourite for the cheeky frog
    Who loves a Christmas snog.
    F is for Fluffy Critter.
    Never be a quitter:
    It makes your mind glitter.
    G is for gin
    That I bought from Flynn.
    Passing it down to my next-of-kin.
    H is for Heineken,
    Sold by the Chinamen,
    And bought by the riflemen.

I is for ice.
Ice is a spice.
Ice makes all drinks nice.
J is for Jack Daniels
Travelling for miles
Filling up the aisles
K is for Kiwi Masquerade.
The glasses are on parade
For emergency hydration aid.
L is for liquor.
This wonderful ichor
Belongs to the vicar.
M is for Malibu
For when you're feeling blue,
And want to feel anew.
N is for Nutty Professor,
Drinking with a hairdresser
And the rainbow jester.
O is for Orange Blossom.
I've heard it's really awesome.
I should try some.
P is for Pina Colada
Consumed in an armada
On the coast of Granada
Q is for Queen Of Mexico.
The Queen's cocktail in Glasgow,
And royalty in Moscow.
R is for Raspberry Twist.
What I hold with my fist
Is the best flavour for anything kissed.
S is for sake,
You won't find in a cafe.

Easily led astray.
T is for Tequila,
As graceful as a ballerina
Inspired by the river Gila.
U is for Ultimate Indulgence.
No point in divulgence.
We want refulgence.
V is for vodka.
This drink deserves an Oscar.
It really is a star.
W is for wine!
Don't be a swine!
That drink is mine!
X is for... well X
Like the ones, you put in a text
Hoping that you don't bump into your ex.
Y is for, "You're barred!"
That's the red card
For eardrums scarred.
Z is for Zombie
I tried it in Dundee:
Ended up in an Irish palm tree.

Vintage Swing

Order champagne showers
    also known as liquid courage
    besides the typewriter
    with more rhythm
    than teenage tunes
    and Gameboy colours
    Dance under a red chair
    and twirling umbrellas
    chill in the bathtub
    put your cocktails down
    by the tiger's hips.
    So put on your lampshades
    and your Minnie mouse tights
    Don't blend in when you are
    born to stand out!

Three Things

A lotus blooms by the empty wineglass.
    The little candles flickers beside them.
    The beauty of the short-lived flame
    Isn't so different to the
    Fate of the petals destined to rot.
    The glass has mood swings
    Either always full
    Or always empty
    It's always all over the place
    Until one day it has enough
    And shatters all over the floor
    It doesn't always end that way
    If you look after the three things
    The candle can last for days
    The flower can last for weeks
    The glass can last forever

Giant Leaves

Giant leaves obey the wind
 Following her waves unto
 The parallel grass
 A modern maiden
 Builds rainbow castles
 For the crawly community
 It doesn't take long
 For the ants to move in
 Slugs lay their eggs below
 The sturdy bricks
 The worm wiggles through
 Seeking shelter from
 The hungry crows
 The landlord can't kick him out
 He's twenty times the size of him.

Happy Ending

The news reeks of death
    Another solider sent home in a casket
    Peaceful protests wiped out my social media
    A war between two parties
    Both with blood on their hands
    A rising star
    Stripped of her shine
    And thrown into obscurity
    Society is going backwards
    And we're being robbed
    From the very people
    We should be able to trust
    They warned us.
    They killed them.
    We won't find happily ever after here
    Nor will be find it at the golden staircase
    Worshipping someone we don't truly know
    It's something that can't be found
    But when you obtain it: you'll know
    Is it too hard to ask for a happy ending?

Pålegg

What is a pålegg?
    In addition to being untranslatable,
    it's not something you'll find in your
    dictionary, so try Google instead.
    A love cupid for two slices of bread
    The magnet that
    holds carbohydrate slabs together.
    The edible ointment that brings bread to life
    Oral love guided by a silver knife.
    Just ask the baker's wife.
    The cucumbers above your eye.
    The pressed tomatoes in your soup.
    A healthy spread of spreadable cheese,
    And bananas from under the trees.
    A lovely Norwegian noun
    that lives in your cupboards
    or stocked up in your fridge
    You know lots of påleggs
    especially those eggs.

The Elderly Painter

An elderly painter
    forgets his
    name
    But never forgets
    old secrets buried
    with a Dalmatian dog
    He's lost the TV remote
    but he never loses
    the loneliness
    The retired counsellor
    and part-time scriptwriter
    has been like this since his Calamity Jane
    PERISHED.

Why it's Grey

It's grey because it's sad.
    The green is dead.
    News from the dead,
    Wild swans perform
    A post-mortem on
    the ninja
    Between an opal sky and dead sky
    Bad girls play the dare game by a red wall.
    Cause of death: a boot to the head.

We Walked

Follow me says the music
    See why the whales come
    In the sleepover secret
    At charm school
    What shall we do?
    We walk
    What else can we do?
    We know the route
    Off by heart

The Flowers of Suicide Forest

These flowers and candles have been planted here,
    for the spirits that roam above and below the Sea of Trees
    sunk deep within their own darkness and despair – their
    cries for help buried too deep for us to hear.
    I write this poem for the ones that have
    or are considering ending their own lives in
    and beyond Aokigahara.
    Your body may be rotten,
    Your soul may be broken,
    but you are still loved.
    You will always be in the thoughts of
    strangers and friends.
    That red flower that flourishes
    through the blood and debris against
    all odds curtsies to the sun –
    It rises for you.
    It's not too late
    To turn around!
    Hello there. You've come to save me.
    Thank you for your concern,
    But I've not come here to die.
    I've come to pay respects
    For the ones that passed

And support the ones
on the edge of suicide

Diet Pills In The View Of An Atheist

I believe in diet pills
as much as I believe
in Jesus Christ and
the man who walked
on the moon

Love is all full

Knock out to time...finished finally download
    memories
    old years ten now is
    eater soul realises you when moment that
    update 21bg frigid
    hopefully will I and thanks
    Love is all full to listening am I
    soon you see and care cool
    translate google bloody

Mother Fluff Was A Diamond

Mother Fluff was a diamond
    butterfly goddess lathering
    in peaches.
    The crystal meth princes
    down tequilas slams and hash cakes
    for breakfast.
    "Blow me," they beg.
    "No," says Mother Fluff as
    she breaks the wooden tables

They Rose

They rose
    like friends
    bitter gods
    and goddesses
    judge them.
    They want
    it all with a
    bed of roses
    it will take a
    lot of work
    for it to come
    true, but it is
    not impossible.
    They will
    win, because
    their hearts
    bodies and
    souls are in it.

Lush Life

It's a lush life when we think about it.
    It might not seem it, but it is a bit.
    We're fortunate to breathe this air,
    To swim these waters and touch
    These beloved plants
    Kindness brings more colour
    It's funny how the ones that
    rule the world have no idea
    how the world works
    let's make the most of everything
    before its spoilt forever

Blue smiles

Mocking
There are no faces
Insulting
They have no hearts
Attacking
My defence is worthless
Banging
Always inside my head
Tripping
Tripping me over again and again
Screaming
I never get sleep
Biting
Holes everywhere
Bleeding
Please just make it stop
Suffering
I don't want to do this anymore

Back to Work

Back to work
    With these
    Tuesday thoughts
    People are backing
    Punish a Muslim day
    It's not just today
    And it's not just Muslims
    The ones that orchestrate
    This growing hate
    Will end up destroying
    The world

Pink Smiles

Engaged
Every day should be like this
Motivated
I'm gonna give it my all
Wholeheartedly
I know I can win gold
Creatively
The ideas never stop
Love
full of soul

Goddamn Perverts

They're everywhere!
    They just don't give up!
    Tell them to fuck off
    And they ask
    What's your bra size?
    The red flags are these,
    They ask for your ASL
    They ask if you're single
    And if you say yes
    They ask if you like them
    Annoying twats!
    No, I don't like you
    We've only just met
    Only five seconds
    To form an opinion
    Sorry, I don't like you
    You're just another one of those goddamn perverts!

Your Game Is Lame

Your game is lame
You can't fight the night
You're as silly as willy
You're needy and greedy
You spite with fright
Your game is lame

What People Think Of Writers

Why people think that all writers
Are loaded with lots of money?
We can't all be bestsellers,
But we're still pretty awesome.
I often look at my bank balance
And cry. ;-;
And look at the prices of the things
I want
And places I want to go
And cry some more. ;-;

A Standoff

A standoff between
The sneezing dog
And the musical cow
The history of Britain
lies in their hands

Red Bubbles

She's a sick and twisted monster
    She slashes her victims without remorse
    And guess what everyone calls her?
    Cuddles!
    With the remains of her victims
    She does all sorts of stuff
    She calls herself an artist
    Grotesque indeed
    Just like Mrs Lovett
    She makes a good kidney pie
    And builds houses with bones
    Like Lego bricks
    And she does it all for free
    "Saves you a fortune on funerals!"
    She cries with glee
    She has a blood bank you see
    Uses all the blood of her victims
    Mixes it with soap
    To form big red bubbles

Long Live the Paper Queen

The march of the paper queen
    involves citizens in green
    holding handwritten rhapsodies
    and a hymn full of lies
    The letter hides the downfall
    Layers of fear injected to all
    Apart from the cat ladies
    protecting the honey and the bees
    Love live the paper queen

Sundays

There's a love/hate relationship with Sundays
    Sunday lay-ins are the best
    Until time zooms so fast
    You're left with the dread
    Of going to work Monday morning
    Saturday night hangovers
    Get no sympathy from Sunday hangovers
    Everything is closed
    And whatever's open
    Closes early
    But it's a nice vibe
    Wheather you're a churchgoer or not
    Sundays are still tranquil

Haikus

Modern slays ancient
guidelines stripped with a new name
Bionic Lotus
A floating city
Plenty of lush swimming pools
A grand holiday
Friends and foreigners
hug trees and kiss the blue seas
I just want to sleep
You must bring sunshine
Red light and land say it well
Don't forget yourself
The moon is sinking
A white path stretches
Beyond a new dawn

Heart-Shaped Glasses

Kitty wears heart-shaped glasses
    A vanilla shade of pink
    Takes her teal handbag and
    Hot pink shoes wherever she goes
    Love is her middle name
    Endlessly wanting to meet her
    Eternity we've been chatting for
    Now the time has come

Pets

It starts with the morning caffeine
    A liquid hug to get me through
    The daily jog and invisible thugs
    The furry relatives that lick your face,
    chew your stuff and sit on you
    Gives you their love.
    My pet is cuter than your pets.

Friday Fries

Everyone likes
fish and chips
on a Friday
wrapped in
newspaper
and grease
covered fake
news that
nobody cares
about. We
just want to
eat our chips
in peace. It's
what keeps
us going in
this post
brexit world
ran by the
tory scum.
They eat their
fish and chips
in golden paper
as they fine the
homeless money

they will never
be able to have.
I hope the fish
bite back and
give them the
shits

How I Can Be A Better Person

Maybe I should lose some weight;
    Thin has and will always be in.
    Maybe I should give up smoking;
    I'm choking with so much sin.
    Maybe I should sign up to the gym;
    I could turn into a muscle machine.
    Maybe I should go on holiday;
    Nobody will believe where I've just been.
    Maybe I should make some friends;
    I could find my brand new twin.

An Open Book

It's not a mess when it's an open book
    It's the exhibition of my imagination
    Flying through a thousand centuries
    The characters I've known loved and lost
    Outnumber the grains of Sahara
    If it was not for the heroes and heroines
    Of my short-lived innocence,
    Then I would not be the person I am today
    Even if I was able to read and memorize
    Every page in all these books
    It would never be enough
    For I know that every day
    Something dies
    Something is born
    Reborn
    Or created
    The knowledge I have now
    Will never be enough
    There is more upon the horizon
    Beautiful forms of words and art
    That is waiting to be discovered

Jungle Influencers

The turtle climbs the tree
    Pretending it's a floating butterfly
    Scrolling up each branch she can see
    Fluorescent wings whizzing by
    In the jungle she has the time
    To think her life is an utter bore
    If she only had at least a dime
    She could grow wings and soar

Beneath a shrinking apple
    Was one trying to sing
    About her fate in a pupa chapel
    The turtle stayed to swing
    I will be gone tomorrow
    The butterfly says as with a smile
    There is no need to feel any sorrow
    As I know my life was worthwhile

There was no time to attempt
    To be something she was not
    Being loved as herself is a rare moment
    Following a fluttering paw by a yacht

The turtle's confidence recovers
Where flowing water is surplus
It is here where she discovers
The turtle has her own purpose

Did you love *Lockdown Poetry*? Then you should read *Drinking Poetry*[1] by Chloe Gilholy!

[2]

Tea or coffee, whichever drink you prefer it fuels the soul. A collection of poems celebrating the delights, tastes and benefits of tea, coffee and alcohol.

---

1. https://books2read.com/u/49Z8Gd

2. https://books2read.com/u/49Z8Gd

Also by Chloe Gilholy

Life With Poetry
Drinking Poetry
Daily Poetry
Living Poetry
Loving Poetry
Travelling Poetry
Lockdown Poetry

Standalone
Fishman
Game of Mass Destruction
Little Horrors
Inbu's Heart
Emerald Oasis

About the Author

Chloe Gilholy is a healthcare worker from Oxfordshire. She published her first poem when she was eight and she hasn't stopped since.